MW00896876

A Woman Used by God

A Woman Used by God

The Spirituality of Mother Mary Lange, OSP

Sr. Magdala Marie Gilbert, OSP

Copyright © 2016 by Sr. Magdala Marie Gilbert, OSP.

ISBN: Softcover   978-1-5144-7638-3
               ebook   978-1-5144-7637-6

All rights reserved. No part of this book may be reproduced or transmitted in any form or by any means, electronic or mechanical, including photocopying, recording, or by any information storage or retrieval system, without permission in writing from the copyright owner or the Oblate Sisters of Providence.

© 2007 by The Franciscan Sisters of Allegany *Illustrations and Designs*

Allegany Arts -Permission given by Sister Dorothy Dwyer, OSF by email.

© 1992 Holy Bible -American Bible Society – Today's English Version

The American Bible Society is glad to grant authors and publishers the right to use up to one thousand(1,000) verses from the Today"s English Version text in church, religious and other publications without the need to seek and receive written permission. However, the extent of quotations must not comprise complete book nor should it amount to more than 50% of the work

Print information available on the last page

Rev. date: 03/23/2016

To order additional copies of this book, contact:
Xlibris
1-888-795-4274
www.Xlibris.com
Orders@Xlibris.com
733218

CONTENTS

To my parents

family

and

OSP congregation

ACKNOWLEDGMENTS

In thanksgiving to God who has given me the insights for this piece of work. Special thanks to Ms. Sharon Knecht, Archivist; Sr. Marcia L. Hall, OSP; and Sr. Trinita Baeza, OSP, for assisting with this manuscript. May God bless them with His abundant graces.

INTRODUCTION

Mother Mary Lange, OSP

A Woman of Faith and Courage

1794-1882

Before Elizabeth Clarissa Lange came to the United States from Santiago de Cuba, she heard the Voice of God. When one hears the Voice of God, it is not to be ignored. Some people call it a vocational call. Whatever Elizabeth Lange was doing or where she was when she heard God's voice, it impelled her to heed it. She eventually found her way to Maryland. I wonder what she was thinking when she heard this call. Getting ready for her journey, Elizabeth had to decide what clothing she would take and she would discard. Hats were worn in those days, and hat boxes would take up lots of space, so she had to decide to give these away as well. Did she have a trunk, or did she use several suitcases? This is not known. My grandmother had a huge trunk that she carried with her whenever she traveled from Texas to Louisiana between her son, my uncle, and her daughter, my mother. This trunk had drawers that held quite a few things. There was even a place for hanging things. I wonder if Elizabeth had a trunk and, if so, if it was like this one. Then again, she may have taken two trunks. Who knows? My next query is, was she planning to just visit, or had she planned on staying? Many of these questions will never be answered of course since Elizabeth was such a no-nonsense person. It may have been a possibility that she was going to go back home to

Cuba to her mother, Annette Lange. It is not certain how she arrived at the ship she would take on the day of her departure. Was there a large entourage to see her off, or were there only close friends and a few relatives?

How many days did it take her to pack and get all of her business in order? Come to think of it, she might have had a small school started in Cuba since she seemed prepared to open a school and apparently knew how to go about it. If she had a school, she had to find someone to continue this ministry. She must have had friends to say farewell to before her journey to the United States, her destination Baltimore, Maryland. I wonder why she chose Baltimore to settle and begin her school. She surely knew that there was slavery in Maryland. Was it Providence leading her?

It would be interesting to know the name of the ship that transported Elizabeth to the shores of the United States. This silent woman left not a clue. It is not even found in any ship log that we can find. How could this be? Were the papers lost through fire or storm? It seems as if Elizabeth was a spirit until after her feet hit the shores of the United States that she took on real form. Until that time to this day, there are no records of her early life. No comprehensive records have been found today, not even the name of the ship she sailed on. She had to come by sea because there were no airplanes that would do that kind of flying during those days. Still here she was a living presence, ready to take on the system.

Nothing is known for certain about the early years of Elizabeth Lange. What we do know is that she appeared on the scene with the force of a small tornado. When she decided to make Jesus her choice, she gave her life totally to God. Getting settled in Baltimore and ultimately starting a school in 1828 and the first permanent black religious congregation in 1829, the first of its kind in the world, was a feat in itself. Anyone who knows the Oblate Sisters of Providence and has read the history or even heard of it knows that Lange met Fr. James Hector Joubert who asked Elizabeth Lange and her companion Marie Magdaleine Balas to start a school to teach the children to read so they could learn to read their catechism. Thus, Father Joubert approached Ms. Lange and asked her to take on this assignment. He was teaching the children their catechism and found they could not read well and therefore were having a problem learning their catechism. In the talking stage, Elizabeth made it known to Father Joubert that she yearned to "consecrate her life to God," and he thought it would be a splendid idea to start a religious order at the same time. So out of this conversation was born the Oblate Sisters of Providence.

What we do know about Lange was that she was a very forceful woman. She knew what she wanted out of life and worked to make her dream a reality. Making dreams a reality was no easy task especially in those days. First she was a foreigner, a woman, a woman of color, a Catholic, and an educator. All of this was against her from the beginning seeing that Maryland was a slave state and slavery was a big part of the society. Slavery had such a stronghold in Maryland that even some sisters and priests of the Catholic Church had slaves. But somehow God was on her side. She worked with them to bring forth

two double firsts. The first was a Catholic school for black children, Saint Frances School for Colored Girls (later it became Saint Frances Academy); and the next was the first permanent congregation of sisters of African descent, the Oblate Sisters of Providence.

Who would have thought that this little foreigner would stir up such ideas in a man's world? No one would have guessed that this phenomenon would take place in Baltimore. Who would

have thought, a black woman starting a congregation, even if she was Catholic. In spite of all odds, the impossible happened. God definitely had a hand in this as voiced by Archbishop James Whitfield of Baltimore who said, "The finger of God is in this." Not only did God had a hand in the congregation, but also God's whole being was in the venture of Elizabeth Lange. Providence did and is still providing for the congregation of the Oblate Sisters of Providence.

Although little is known about the early life of Elizabeth Lange, all things are possible if we allow God to use us as Elizabeth allowed God to use her. It makes no difference when or where Elizabeth originated, whether Cuba or Haiti, or whether she had been in the States, went back to Cuba, and returned to the States. All of that is irrelevant, but what we do know at this moment is what matters most. First of all, we know that she was a real person who came to the United States, founded a school and a congregation, and continued to grow in holiness. Her body was interred in the New Cathedral Cemetery, and her death certificate can be found in the hall of records in Baltimore as well as in the archives of the Oblate Sisters. *The photo of the sisters seen in this section can be found in the archives of the Oblate Sisters of Providence.*

On May 28, 2013, Mother Lange's body, buried in the New Cathedral Cemetery, was exhumed and brought to the Oblate Motherhouse on June 3, 2013, amid much thanksgiving and joy. Many filed in procession to view the remains of Mother Lange before she was placed in the sarcophagus and sealed. Now those devoted to Mother Lange may come and pray or just meditate on the life of this wonderful woman.

A LISTENING HEART

Lange heard God's call
From the deep recesses of her heart.

Lange heard God's call.
She was a woman who gave all
To the cause she was called to do
By building up the kingdom too
Lange heard God's call.

CHALLENGES

Challenges are all around us.
Causing us to choose every day,
That which would suit us thus
As we walk the life of faith.

Challenges urge us to grasp
Concepts that lift us high.
High beyond the ordinary situation
Encountered in daily living.

Challenges lift us above the mundane.
Leading us to grapple with crises
That arise as we develop spiritually,
Leading us to greater fidelity.

Challenges caused Mother Mary Lange
To grasp the significance of dedication.
She wanted to give total self-immolation,
In becoming a religious sister.

Challenges spurred her onward
To become that chosen person God deemed,
Her to be as a bride of Christ
And as an Oblate Sister of Providence.

PREFACE

Elizabeth Clarissa Lange, the Woman

A.k.a.

Mother Mary Lange, OSP

An

Oblate Sister of Providence

As was stated in the introduction, very little is known about the early life of Elizabeth Clarissa Lange. What we do know is that she was a real flesh-and-blood person. Nor do we know what sort of life she lived before she met the Sulpicians. Little is known for certain about Elizabeth until she showed up in Baltimore in her early or late twenties. The first evidence we have shows that she was in Baltimore in 1812.

We have census records, obituaries, and an account written by Sr. Therese Willigmann, an Oblate who lived with Mother Lange for over forty years. Even then we know little about her life in Baltimore until she became an Oblate Sister of Providence.

This book is not about the early years of the life of Elizabeth Lange. It is about the spirituality of Elizabeth Lange (Mother Mary) as she lived this life as an Oblate Sister of Providence. It is about her spiritual growth as she led her little congregation, her spiritual development, her dedication to God, her charism, and the legacy she left for the congregation that she founded along with three other spirit-filled, God-fearing women, namely, Marie Magdaleine Balas (Sister Mary Frances), Rose Boegue (Sister Mary Rose), Almaide Maxis Duchemin (Sister Mary Theresa), and Fr. James Hector Joubert, SS, on July 2, 1829. All else pales in comparison to this historic event, and as some would so glibly say, "And the rest is history." Lange's hunger for God led her on the path she took. She had a mandate from God, and she had to fulfill it.

TO HUNGER

To hunger for God is so awesome
The soul yearns to be totally united
To the source of its being.

Mary Lange yearned for God;
Her soul would not rest until
It worked in the service of God.

Many, many years passed before
This dream became an actuality.
She never stopped relying on the Lord.

Her legacy to us is to keep our hands
In the hands of the Creator,
The giver of all good gifts.

1

ദ്ധ൞൞ൕൟ൞

Intentional Living
of
Mary Lange, OSP—Servant of God

What is intentional living? Intentional living is simply personal transformation; you make up your mind to do something and then do it. One's life is centered on some specific aspect. For Mother Lange, the transformation began when she first thought of becoming a religious. Whenever that was, we do not know for sure. It must have been in the back of her mind for a very long time because when approached by Father Joubert, a Sulpician, to open a school for "colored girls" (many of whom were of Haitian descent) and to form a religious community, she said that she had been thinking about consecrating her life to God for about ten years. We can see from this that she had already begun this special spirituality of hers. She must have prayed a long time, and God finally answered her prayer. Prayer is so important in the life of any Christian woman or man, especially those wanting a special union with God. This union has to be intentional.

Thus, on July 2, 1829, the little congregation was founded. Each sister took another name to signify her total giving of self to God as well as to follow in the footsteps of that saint and to ask that the saint be with her as a dedicated religious.

What's in a name, you might ask? In reading the story of John the Baptist on the Feast of the Birth of John the Baptist, the fact that God had given him a name before he was born was significant. While his father, Zachariah, was doing his priestly duty in the temple one day, he was visited by an angel of the Lord. The angel told him that he was to have a son, and this child was to be named John. The name John means "God is gracious." Elizabeth was the name Annette Lange gave her daughter at birth. The name means "God's promise." I suppose God wanted Mother Lange to have a special name when she made her vows on July 2, 1829, for she was inspired to take the name of Mary, which means "Beloved." In changing her name to simply Mary, Mother Lange showed how much she regarded the name of the Virgin Mary, this woman who said yes to God, this beloved woman who would not deny God anything. It was a known fact among the sisters how much Mother Lange loved Mary, the mother of Jesus.

John the Baptist was sent to earth by God to prepare the way for the coming of Christ. Mary Lange, although she did not know it at that time, was sent to Baltimore by God to prepare the way for women of color to become religious women, to spread the Word to the People of God, especially children. Through the preaching of John, many were converted from their sinful ways to prepare their souls for the "Great Day" of the Messiah. Lange was to prepare the minds of children and ultimately adults to accept the teaching of Christ through the medium of education.

Imitating others who have done great feats has spurred women and men throughout the ages to follow suit and become great and courageous leaders themselves. Relying on her namesake Mary, the mother of Jesus, Mother Lange forged ahead. The life of the Virgin Mary was not a bed of roses. She was a poor woman, living in a society where women had no power at all. Like Mary, Mother Lange was poor and was held in little or no esteem as women were held in the time of Mary, the mother of Jesus. Mary Lange took her cue from Mary and put all her trust in God and went about her life doing what she was born to do, become the best she could be, to be a saint.

Gaining strength from her namesake, Mother Lange went about her work relying on the grace of God to see her through the trials of religious life. Although stoning had been abolished when Mary Lange was coming along, something worse was there to taunt her all the while she lived. This was the scourge of racism and rejection not only from the secular society but also from the people of the faith she embraced. When God gives us a name we have to live up to, we need to pay attention and strive to be all we can be for those whom God has given us charge. God will never abandon us to our own demise but will make for us a "way out of no way."

AN ANCHOR

Mary Lange was like an anchor;
She was like a ship set steadfast to the shore.
Her anchor was Jesus, the enhancer.
She looked to him for all things and more.

Mary Lange was like a lover;
Her heart was full of her Lord.
No hatred to bring her down to that level
Placing her hand in God's hand was not hard.

Mary Lange was like a lily planted by a stream,
There nurtured by God, she grew and grew strong.
Her heart expanding to embrace sweet dreams,
Sending roots deep and embracing other prongs.

This woman of God suffered much to teach.
Despite the traumas in life she endured.
Leaving all in God's capable hand to reach,
Finding solace in the cross of the Master secured.

Many did not think too highly of black women wearing the holy habit in the slave state of Maryland. When times became tough after the death of Father Joubert in 1843, Archbishop Samuel Eccleston did nothing to encourage the sisters to continue. But Mary Lange and her sisters carried on. Mother Lange and the sisters had total trust in the Providence of God, and so they continued.

The sisters took in boarders, worked as domestics at Saint Mary's Seminary in Baltimore, made vestments, and helped tend the sick during the time of the cholera. Mother Lange was about serving God at any level.

Throughout her life, we can see that intentional living was lived out daily. Mother Mary Lange lived a life of total dedication and generosity to God and God's people. All that she did was summed up in her own words: "Our sole wish is to do the will of God." This wish is demonstrated in certain characteristics of heroic sanctity that calls us to emulate and imitate: Providence Spirituality founded in and relying upon a loving Providence revealed in a deep, personal relationship with God and a manifest love, trust, and respect for all. Mother Mary lived the conviction that God is true to His word.

Mother Lange did not let the fact that no one of her own race was a religious sister. She did not allow the fact that her own people in the country of her ancestors had been fighting racism and slavery and that she had embraced a country that was doing the same thing. She did not allow herself to be daunted by racial hatred by her own Church leaders who themselves owned slaves and bought into the concept that blacks could be enslaved because they had no souls. She knew she had a soul and that this soul was precious in the sight of her God.

Mary Lange could have been a bitter woman, wanting to get back at those who shunned her who deemed her unworthy to wear a habit like the white sisters in the Church. No, she intentionally fostered love for all her sisters and brothers. She saw the need and intentionally went about seeing that children and orphans were cared for properly.

Because she was an intentional woman, she looked at life through the eyes of Jesus Christ, her Savior. She formed a good attitude that transcended racism or bigotry. Her aim was to do all for the sake of the kingdom, and she could not allow human feelings to get in her way. Mother Mary lived the conviction that God is true to His word. He would care for her, as He cared for all His children. This Providence Spirituality is manifested through the faith and trust that God has provided, does provide, and will provide.

Mary Lange taught her sisters to be intentional in their interaction with the world. Hatred had no place in Mother Lange's heart or that of her sisters. They hung on to the hands of Providence for all their needs. She taught the sisters as well as the students that working for God would have its own reward and to keep their eyes fixed on Jesus, the prize. Mother Lange knew that there would be a special place in heaven for them if they kept the pace and finished the race. Saint Paul stated it well in (1 Corinthians 9:24): "Do you not know that the runners in the stadium all run the race, but only one wins the race? Run as to win." Mother Lange took these words to heart and ran the race successfully to the end.

As her little community grew, Mary Lange could have found ways to retaliate against those who had belittled her in her early years of foundation, but she left the vengeance to God. Her attitude has helped us today to deal with the ups and downs of life. That getting back at others is not the answer but total faith in God, who knows what we are going through and will guard and guide us, if we obeyed as Mother Lange did. If we want to live an authentic Christian life, we have to let go of grudges or hatred of any kind. Easy to do, no . . . but with the grace of God, all things are possible.

A good leader knows how to lead with caution and good judgment. They think things through and then act on the decision. They do not lead others into an ambush but spy out the territory to see that all is safe. That was Mother Lange in her intentional living modality. She did not do this all alone but armed herself with the armor of God.

Mother Lange had a personal relationship with Jesus. This allowed her to do the things she did in the time that she did them. She allowed Jesus to lead the way; she walked behind Jesus. There is a song in the *Lead Me, Guide Me* hymnal #168 called "Lead Me, Guide Me," by Doris Akers, that says, "Lead me, Guide me along the way, for if you lead me, I cannot stray, Lord let me walk each day with thee. Lead me, O Lord lead me." I can imagine that if Mother Lange had that song in her lifetime, she would have said that it was written just for her. Intentional living is not easy, but if you do it daily, your life will change, and you can truly say the first few lines of the hymn "Lead Me" with conviction. The spirituality of Mother Lange lives on in the lives of her sisters who try to follow in the footsteps of their holy foundress.

Mary Lange had a deep love not only for Jesus but also for the Father and the Holy Spirit. She knew that the wisdom with which she would need to sustain her little community had to be filled with the fruits of the Holy Spirit. When we say Providence, we are talking about God the Father, God the Son, and God the Holy Spirit. No Spirituality would be complete without this "Three in One" in our lives, each with their own specific charism. She has left this legacy of reliance on Providence to her congregation, the Oblate Sisters of Providence.

Mother Lange's spirituality has filtered down to her sisters as they go throughout the days, weeks, months, and years with a total trust on Divine Providence. There is a banner in the convent that says, "Providence rises before the sun." And so it does. Her daughters try to keep their eyes on the goal, union with the Trinity.

LOVING GOD

Loving God was not an option
For this daughter of faith.
God instilled in Lange's soul
A fire that blazed as she grew.

From a young girl to the teens
Lived a love that would not die
Undaunted and unrequited
The love of God did abide.

God's love manifested itself
Each day that she taught
A child to love God in the
Way that she ought.

Forgiving grave sin of folks
Each day in the marketplace
The church, communion rail,
The taking of the veil and race.

2

CRITICAL: ❦

Being True to Self

One day, I was listening to EWTN, a Catholic TV station; and one of the priests was speaking about being who you are and being true to self. This was Mother Mary Lange as she lived her life being true to self. She did not care what people said or thought about her. She was convinced that God was her stronghold and would be with her in all that she undertook. Working for God, for Lange, was a pleasure and not a chore.

Elizabeth Clarissa Lange, even before she became a religious as a girl and young woman, must have been on fire for God. She brought this fire with her when she finally fulfilled her dream of becoming a religious. Being on fire for God means that you have to let go of self and cling to God alone. This reliance solely on God in no way kept Mary Lange from being herself. On the contrary, it is a plus for her because with her free will, she decided to follow Jesus but retained her right to be herself in light of her baptism. Mary Lange did not do things in a wishy-washy fashion. All of her religious life was steeped in her providential God.

Mother Lange lived her life longing for total union with the Lord. She was herself, not imitating others, just being true to self. She could have lost heart when rejected by the established society, Church leaders, and religious and laity alike. Being undaunted by ill-treatment, gossip, and innuendoes, she used these rebuffs to bring her closer to God. She really got the message when the Lord said, "Whoever does not take up her/his cross and follow me is not worthy of me" (Matt. 10:38). Following Jesus and His precepts gave Mary Lange a freedom that no one could take from her.

Mother Lange's life was not a path of peace and tranquility. She used her circumstances to find peace and true happiness as she walked hand in hand with her Lord and Savior, Jesus Christ. Looking at her life of service, we can see Mother Lange emulating this saying in the scripture (Mark 10:21): "Go sell everything you own, and then come follow me." She took these words literally and gave her all to follow Christ. Once her mind was made up, Mother Lange never looked back. She gathered students around her, young and old alike, and taught them the tenets of the faith as well as reading, writing, arithmetic, and the arts. Mother Lange's life was a book for all to read. Her life was a living example of an evangelizer. Following her example, her little community spread the faith to various parts of the United States as well as Cuba. Her daughters later extended the work to Central America.

Many Oblate missions closed, but when one door closed, another opened. All one has to do is to be open to the movement of the Holy Spirit and all will be well. Mother Lange was always open to the workings of the Holy Spirit, just as the Spirit guided the small fledgling Church during the time of the apostles and is still working with the Church and each of us today.

Mother Mary Lange continues to intercede to God for all who pray through her intercession and especially her spiritual daughters. Throughout her life, Mary Lange was true to herself and her God. She was herself under all circumstances in good times and in bad times, leaning on Jesus, her Lord.

Let her life of faithful conviction of God's love and guidance carry us to that Promised Land where all will be peace. Let us be ourselves, knowing that being true to God will reap us great rewards, as it did Mother Mary Lange.

HEART ON FIRE

Candles are lit every day
In the hearts of
Those who
Really love God.

Mary Lange's heart was lit
Like a candle each day
As she partook of the
Sacred Host.

Walking the streets of Baltimore
She lit the candles
Of those gone out,
By her word and deeds.

NO EASY STREET

Being colored in Baltimore was no cup of tea
Back then you were always wary of protocol.
Wonder if this is right or that is right.
Some did not know if they were black or white.

It was tough in those days being thought free
But actually not in the eyes of white society.
You had to watch your step, "or so it's said."
Or the slave catchers could steal you, "so it's said."
Being colored in Baltimore was no cup of tea.

Mother Lange knew the risk of this setting
As she set out to follow the call of the Master.
Nothing would deter her from this goal
Although being a religious was no easy street.
Back then you were always wary of protocol.

Joubert and Lange hung out an awful lot.
They talked and they talked far into the night
For some solution to this plight of theirs.
A quickly solvable solution it was not.
Wonder if this is right or that is right.

The "People of God" had to be reckoned with
Win their approval or spin in the dust.
God had no say in this matter of race
Many thought the venture not of good taste.
Some did not know if they were black or white.

3

⊂ℨℬℴℬℴℭℜⅭℨℬℴ

A Woman of Courage

When we look at the life and legacy of Mother Mary Lange, we sometimes forget the fact that when she came to the United States, she was entering another world, a world where slavery was still flourishing. Bounty hunters were still hunting runaway slaves and sometimes enslaving innocent free blacks. Blacks had no one to really fend for them except some churchmen and abolitionists. Others couldn't really care less, because they did not think that blacks had souls. If one could justify that a being had no soul, then they could do with them whatever they chose. Thus was the state of the United States and especially Maryland, a slave state at that time. We must remember that Mother Lange with the help of Father Joubert founded the Oblates thirty-two years before slavery was abolished. Thirty-two years is a long time to survive in a hostile environment. It took a lot of courage and trusting in God. She must have been familiar with (Psalm 27:14), which says, "Wait on the Lord with courage, be stouthearted and wait on the Lord."

Mother Mary Lange understood the concept of waiting on the Lord with courage, especially being a woman in a man's world. She knew hardship firsthand, what it meant to be a tad bit hungry, be without the basic necessities that most people required, like a doctor ready to help her and the children of the house, and enough money so that she and the sisters would not have to work outside the convent.

Mother Lange could resonate with women of the third world who have little modern necessities. She embraced the poor who had little or no voice in society then or now. The destitute, those people, who, like the poor, are considered dispensable commodities, of little worth, and whose rights are not considered.

Mother Lange walked in the path of saints and martyrs. All martyrs are not killed. This was a living martyr who allowed God to use her in His own way. Mother Lange allowed God to use her then, as He is using her now, to bring others to Christ by her witness even in death. Lange followed this bit of wisdom as she struggled to live out Gospel values following in the footsteps of Jesus.

This courageous, resilient woman is a woman for all times. She has something to teach each generation. Anyone can imitate her reliance on Divine Providence, her humility, her sanctity, and her preferential option for the poor. Having a preferential option for the poor was not just words to Mother but a reality that she undertook for the sake of the kingdom.

THIS WOMAN

Mother Mary Lange was no quitter.
She faced up to her dissenter, without a jitter
Stood steadfast to her conviction, so proudly
Unsafe for a black woman to disagree publicly.

Backed by her God and a good friend,
She bucked the system to the very end.
Started a school, which was risky at best.
Was she trying to put God to the test?

Such a fine spiritual woman was she.
Stood up for her right to be free,
Free to be as other Church folk with equality
As she fought to gain some stability.

Bowing down to no one on this earth,
Undaunted, she prayed for all she was worth.
She carried her congregation with humility
Up to the heights of credibility and respectability.

Through good times and through bad times too,
Her reliance on Providence never wavered a sou.
Humbly relying solely on her God,
To hold her hands . . . in spite of all odds.

AMAZING GRACE

(Free Verse)

Amazing grace that worked like fire
Set the heart of Lange ablaze
Her humble heart not filled with ire.

God wrapped his arms around her
Like a mantle and a shield
No taint followed her but sweet myrrh.

Although life was hard and rough
She saw the pitfalls and the strife;
Caught God's hand and stood real tough.

4

ෆ෦ෆ෦ෆ෦ඦ෦

Walking in the Footsteps of Jesus . . .

Mary Lange, a True Evangelizer

We say that Mother Lange was holy, an educator, a woman of vision, a woman ahead of her time, and so she was. As Jesus was the first evangelizer, so Mother Lange walked in His path of holiness, as did the apostles who evangelized after Jesus. They say that an evangelizer is one who lives a simple life unflappable and undaunted by the things of this world. Things are only a means to an end, not the end itself. Mother Lange knew the difference between these two concepts.

It is said that one of the criteria of a true evangelizer; is a person who has a spirit of prayer, a spirit of charity, for all women, men and children. The person must be obedient to God, living a life of humility, self-sacrifice, and denial. A true evangelizer must have a love for the Gospel and the Eucharist. One must have the ability to foster peace and unity among all. A true evangelizer must be willing to proclaim the Good News no matter the harm to oneself. Mother Lange did all of these things. We have heard Mother Lange plied with many names, but few have called her an evangelizer.

Many talk about the new evangelization, that it is not only the priest or the minister who has this duty to evangelize. This call to evangelize is the duty of all baptized Christians; it is for all the faithful. Mother Lange was ahead of her time. She was doing her evangelical work from the time she said yes to God and found herself reaching out to the poor and disenfranchised in Baltimore, Maryland, and the surrounding area. Although she began in Baltimore, through her Oblates, she has left her mark around the United States, Cuba, Puerto Rico, and Costa Rica. Now that Mother has been deemed "Servant of God" by the Church, she is still doing the work she began over 180 years. She is known around the world in over sixteen countries.

Mother Lange reminds us of Saint Theresa, the Little Flower, who is called Patron of the Missions, although she never left her convent in France. Mother Lange fulfilled the admonition of Saint Paul to Timothy (2 Tim. 4:5): "But you, be self-possessed in all circumstances; put up with hardship; perform the work of an evangelist; fulfill your ministry." Mother Lange did that and much, much more. Little did Lange know the effect that her yes to God would achieve.

But as we look around us, we see how effort witnessing and being a willing vessel in the hand of God can do for those who will allow God to mold and fashion them. Mother Lange allowed God to mold and fashion her like the potter molds and fashions a lump of ordinary clay into a rare piece of art. I am sure it was not easy having a strong will and bending it to the will of another. However, that is what makes a saint, doing what we do not like for the love of God, knowing that in the end everything will be all right. Pounding the sidewalks of the streets of Baltimore was no easy task, but her tenacity paid off like the star in the sky: although hidden, it continues to shine and sparkle. Evangelization is stepping out of our comfort zone and treading deep waters. Mother Lange treaded deep waters and reaped a bountiful harvest for God.

SHE PRAYED

(Senryu)

Rose early each day
To ask her God for His strength
And blessing once again.

Holding on to God
Mother Lange saw what could be,
Took the risk and tried.

Did what she had to,
To keep her congregation
On its path to God.

Unafraid to work,
Wash, and iron to meet the needs
Of community.

WOMAN OF INTEGRITY

(Etheree)

Lange,
Simple
Pioneer
Woman of faith
Loved the truth always
In spite of grueling odds
This brave woman held to her
Principles when told to go home.
She put hope and trust in her dear God,
Knowing that Providence would fill all needs.

5

Honoring the Vows as a Religious Mother Lange Embraced Chastity

Mother Lange totally embraced the life she chose for herself. Now that she was a vowed religious, she took the vows of chastity, poverty, and obedience seriously. Although Mother Lange loved children—this was proven by the fact that before she became a sister, she had a school of her own—she decided to forgo motherhood for Jesus. She chose the life of celibacy. She did not allow herself to entertain marriage and have a family. Her longing for union with Jesus was her goal. The Church, the children in her charge, and friends would now occupy her life. To her, this was better than family, since she could have it all. Mother Lange had a balanced relationship with God. She saw God, people, and things as a unit, forever united to give the world its proper balance. Many in white society, at that time, felt that people of color could not live chaste lives. This is probably the reason they gave the sisters such a hard time. But Mother Lange knew who her Lord was and intended to follow Jesus. This Jesus, who was God, had not a blemish on His soul. As a true follower of Jesus, she took hold of celibacy and never let it go. Her theme song could well have been "All to Jesus I surrender / All to him I freely give" (from the *Lead Me, Guide Me* hymnal #162). There is another hymn written by Dan Schulte, SJ, which could also have been her theme song. This hymn called "Here I Am, Lord" can also be found in the *Lead Me, Guide Me* hymnal #283.

Mother Lange Embraced

Poverty

She perfectly understood the vow of poverty. Although she had plenty of money from her family, she did not hold on to it as if it were hers alone. She lived her life as if she had none. Lange used the money she had to help others, her small congregation, and her charges, "the children of the house." She embraced poverty as did Saint Francis of Assisi. It was not something she adored, but she used it as a means to do something good. It was to be used for the honor and glory of God. Money, to her, was a stepping stone on her journey to becoming like Jesus. Jesus was so poor that the Bible states that He had nowhere to lay His head. He totally depended on others for His needs. When Mother Lange's money was gone, she also relied on others to help her in her mission.

She read the Bible and took note on what it said, that "money is the root of all evil." She knew that total detachment was her only option for striving to be like Jesus. She realized that she had more on this earth than Jesus did, while he was on earth. Jesus did not have a thing to call his own. Lange felt it a privilege to imitate Jesus in her new life.

As a religious, she would have to share everything, own nothing, to be a pauper as it were. She would have to share a room for the rest of her life, have special times to get up, go to bed, and eat. Her whole life would be regulated. She would have to ask permission to spend money, get permission to give anything away.

Mother Lange Embraced

Obedience

Obedience, one would imagine, would be hard for Mother Lange, for she was a woman who knew what she wanted and went about getting it with her whole being. She knew, however, that if she wanted to walk side by side with Jesus, she had to fashion her will to that of Jesus. She could no longer be her own "boss" but had to surrender her will to that of the Holy Spirit.

It is a known fact that people who want something bad enough will do just about anything to get it. Mother Lange was running for the "prize," heaven. The only way to get there was God's way. She knew it was not going to be easy. She saw this in her encounter with the Church and other folks. However, she never turned back or was ever heard to say that this was too hard. She took the bullet in her teeth and walked on. Her whole life would be regulated. When in a room at community recreation, she would also have to ask permission to leave the room.

Mother Lange had to pray a lot. She had to invoke the Father, the Son, and the Holy Spirit, if she was to continue this life of an obedient religious. Religious life during her time was no bed of roses, for even roses have thrones. Mother Lange had a hotline to the Triune God. She spent her whole life acquiescing to Divine inspirations. That is why she could say, "Our sole wish is to do the will of God." From the "legacy" that she left the Oblate Sisters and others, it is evident to this day how her faithfulness to the will of God shaped her life and those close to her.

As a religious, Mother Lange had to follow the rules of the Church for the religious. She had to obey the rules like everyone else, no exemptions because she was superior. Of course it was her duty to see that everyone kept the rules. She set the example for them. Mother Lange was like any other sister in the convent. Even when leaving the room if the sisters were all assembled, she had to ask permission to leave the room. She had to ask even if it was to go to the restroom. Obedience was serious business in those days.

Mother Lange is a hard act to follow. Anyone following in her footsteps and serious about being a religious must be serious about her vocation.

GOD'S WOMAN

Mary Lange was a woman of God,
Lowly yet steeped in the
Knowledge of
Scripture.

Scripture was where she heard
The Master's call
Deep in the heart of the
Caribbean
And the United States.
The United States where
her meditation,
Prayers,
And yearning
Became a reality.

A reality of total service
To this God
She deeply loved
And the people
Entrusted to her.

6

Mother Mary Lange and the Blessed Virgin Mary

We recommend this important affair to our good Mother.

—Mother Mary Lange

"We recommend this important affair to our good Mother." We can see from this statement that Mother Mary Lange had great devotion to Mary, the mother of Jesus. She knew that Mary was a good mother and would deny her child nothing. Being the mother of Jesus, Mary became automatically our mother too. Thus, Mother Lange relied heavily on Mary to guide her and her small congregation. She did not hesitate to remind the sisters that Mary was an important person in her life and therefore could be central in the lives of the sisters as well.

After making their retreat to become sisters on July 2, 1829, Elizabeth Clarissa Lange took the name of Mary. She did not add any other name to this. She was simply Sister Mary. It became a custom of the sisters to change their name to their favorite saint and to have the name Mary prefixed to this name at their investiture as novices. After Vatican II, sisters were allowed to go back to their baptismal names if they wished. Many of the sisters chose to retain their given religious names with Mary affixed to it. Although the sisters do not affix Mary to their names anymore, the Oblate Sisters of Providence still have great respect and devotion to Mary, the mother of Jesus.

Mother Lange prayed to Mary many, many times, especially during the baby steps of the small congregation. Because times were not easy in the slave state of Maryland, she knew that she could not totally rely on anyone earthly to help her except God through the intercession of Mary. Mother Lange must have used the statement "We recommend this important affair to our good Mother" often when she and the sisters were in dire need or when she needed direction to make a wise decision. This statement was relevant to Mother Mary then and is relevant to the Oblate Sisters and all who believe in her cause today and hopefully beyond.

Since Mother Lange had a great devotion to Mary, the mother of Jesus, she and the sisters fostered a great devotion to the rosary. It is the custom, even to this day, to say the rosary daily, following the devotion of the foundress in her devotion to Mary. So it would seem fitting that Mother Lange would go to Mary when she or the congregation needed God's assistance. We all know that Jesus can refuse His mother nothing. Mother Lange was wise in her dealings with the Godhead. In (John 2:1–8), we see at the wedding feast of Cana that Jesus could not refuse to act for His mother even though He said that his time had not come; but for the love of the Mother, His mission, it seemed, was hastened because of the request of Mary.

The evidence of the sisters' devotion to Mary even now is seen through their daily prayers. At the end of all their prayers, they end with this prayer: "We fly to thy patronage, O Holy Mother of God, despise not our petitions in our necessities but deliver us from dangers,

O ever glorious and blessed virgin. Amen." The sisters have a great devotion to our Lady of Providence. In fact, the Motherhouse Convent is called Our Lady of Mount Providence. Thank you, Mary, our mother, for continuing to watch over and protecting the daughters of Mother Mary Lange.

SAYING YES, TO GOD

When God calls, you must follow.
It is not "if" you will follow . . . you must.

We are not here to do our will
But that of the Master Craftsman's.
When God calls, you must follow.

Life is bearable when we kneel in reverent awe
Of the will of God in our lives.
It is not "if" you will follow . . . you must.

A MOTHER

A mother is a unique person.
They kiss scraped knees,
Soothe sobbing tears,
Hurt feelings
And.
Headaches.

They tuck you in bed at night
And read you good stories
Your every need is met
By this wonderful,
Beautiful woman
Called . . .
Mother.

Such was Mother Mary Lange's position
To each of her sisters in Christ.
Although not children
As such,
Her motherly compassion
And love was
The very
Same
Thing.

7

Mother Mary Lange and Prayer

Prayer is the DNA of the spiritual life.

I

Because of the time in which she lived, Mother Lange had to have a firm and deep spiritual life. She took to heart Saint Paul's admonition to the Colossians, (Col. 4:2): "Persevere in prayer, being watchful in it with thanksgiving." To persevere in prayer is to be watchful in it with thanksgiving. The word "persevere" meant a lot to Mother Lange, for she knew that to do what God wanted from her, she had to be always prayed up. All of us know the definition of perseverance. Don't give up, be steadfast, and stay strong in spite of difficulty. In prayer, it means to never give up no matter what. It means being consistent in what you pray for, and when you receive what you ask for, be sure to thank God for the favor.

Sometimes God takes His good time in answering some prayers. I suppose we have all experienced that at one time or another. Look at Saint Monica, the mother of Saint Augustine. She prayed for thirty years for her wayward son to come to God. Had she given up, we would not have that great saint with all his wealth of spiritual writings, especially *Confessions* and *City of God*, making up—it seemed—for lost time. While God seemed not to be listening, Saint Monica's prayers were finally answered. She must have spent the rest of her life thanking God for this great favor.

Mother Mary Lange prayed for ten years for God to show her a way to consecrate her life to God. As we have seen in other passages, after she became a sister, she met all kinds of difficulties from one obstacle or another. Life was not easy in those days; still, she did not give up. Many of us would not have put up with the situation. However, because she persevered in prayer, relying totally on the providence of God, He heard her plea. It was not easy living in a hostile environment. It must have been quite scary. However, she was undaunted in her resolve. She was a praying woman who waited on the Lord. When we pray and wait on the Lord, anything is possible, as it was for Mother Lange. The operative phrase here is "persevering in prayer." Mother Lange did that—always thanking God for another new day to serve by going about her daily task, knowing that God was always with her and her charges. She had to have been a woman of prayer.

Prayer, it is said, is the lifting of the mind and heart to God. It is taking our ordinary circumstances in life and giving it to God. It takes time, meditation, and some idea of "WHO" this God is . . . God has to be someone personal, as personal as the skin on our bodies. Prayer, Mother Lange knew, was about relationship, having a special personal relationship with her God.

Mother Lange knew long ago that in order for her and her little community to survive, she had to have a very close relationship with God. She knew somehow that becoming close to Jesus was one of the prerequisites for becoming holy. Things did not always go the way Mother Lange thought they should go, but still, she hung on to Jesus. She knew that to persevere meant to cling to God even when the situation did not make any sense.

II

It is said that Mother Lange had a great devotion to Jesus in the Most Blessed Sacrament. She had a great devotion to her daily prayers. It is unknown whether she used other forms of prayers, but it is possible that she not only did private meditation but was also very intentional in having Jesus always in her thoughts during the day. Today there are various places where one can go to pray in private. Mother did not have the luxury of taking a nature walk or sitting by a stream to meditate or having access to a labyrinth or outside Stations of the Cross.

Mother Lange was aware that God knows each of us and does not need an introduction. He does want us to talk to Him often, and this talking is known as prayer. Most women know what it is like to have a girlfriend that you like very much. When you come from work or shopping, you would immediately get on the telephone and start talking as if you had not seen each other for days. That's the kind of relationship God wants with us and which Mother Lange had with her God.

In the Bible, there are so many instances where people persevered in prayer, where they were faithful to it. In the Old Testament, there were Abraham, Moses, Jeremiah, Elijah, David, Hannah, Deborah, Naomi, Ruth, other prophets, holy men and women, all who had a personal relationship with God. Mother Lange must have loved the story of Hannah, the mother of Samuel (1 Sam. 1:28). Unable to have children, Hannah prayed and prayed; in fact, she prayed so much that the prophet Eli thought that she was drunk. Finally, God gave her the son for which she begged and pleaded. She was so grateful to God that in total thanksgiving she gave her son Samuel for the service of the temple. For ordinary people, God does not expect such a great sacrifice like Hannah, but He does expect religious women and men to do some sacrificing.

In the New Testament (Mark 5:25–30), a woman with a blood problem was cured just by touching the hem of Jesus's garment. Also in (Mark 7:24-30), the Syrophoenician woman whose daughter was possessed by a demon and who was insulted by being called a dog begged relentlessly for her daughter's healing. Lange, like her, was undaunted by any rebuke.

Mother Lange prayed to God with confidence. She let go, emptied herself of self, and allowed God to be God, being unafraid. Lange approached the throne of God boldly with all of her petitions, knowing that God is a loving God; sinful though we may be, yet God will not disappoint us because we are His children. It did not seem that Lange was intimidated by God and became distressed because she thought she should not address God in a familiar fashion, being fearful that her prayers would not be heard. She knew we should have great trust in God, in spite of our weakness and sin. God wants only what is best for us, and God does not care about the multiplicity of our words.

Lange talked to God as a friend. Her legacy to us too is to pray with sincerity and to tell God what we are asking for is important, that we know He heard our prayer and we will await His answer with humility and trust.

Mother Lange's life should teach us that sometimes we pray for certain things like a mother praying for her daughter who had cancer, but the daughter died anyway. This unanswered prayer brings confusion and pain. The mother might ask God why He did not heal her daughter. At other times when people disappoint us, we have a hard time praying. Sometimes we are disappointed with ourselves and cannot pray like we want, so we put it off. In all these situations, God cares . . . All we have to do is persevere even when all seems lost or futile.

Prayer, Mother Lange knew, not only allows us to experience God but also allows others to experience God through us. We become Christ to others daily because of our union with Jesus in the Eucharist. We go to communion and in our thanksgiving prayer say, "Let others see you in me, Jesus," and Jesus becomes Eucharist to all we meet. All of this is prayer. Jesus taught us well how to pray. In (Luke 11:1–4), the apostles wanted to pray as the disciples of John prayed. So they asked Jesus to teach them how to pray. Jesus said, "'s how you are to pray . . ." and taught them the Our Father. Lange too learned to pray as the apostles. She took the admonition of Jesus to pray in secret, to not be a show-off, and to pray from the heart with God as the main focus.

Persevering in prayer, God blessed Mother Lange and her sisters to do great things for Him and the people of God. So through prayer, Mother Lange's life had a great effect on the lives of those who have crossed her path before she died and continued through the congregation she founded. In (1 Thessalonians 5:17), we are admonished to pray without ceasing. We can do this by intentionally placing ourselves always in the presence of God. Like Mother Lange, we walk with God . . . we talk with God . . . everywhere we go, even when we are having fun . . . when we are serious . . . when we are driving . . . when we are talking to our best friend. This way we always feel God's presence in our lives. You might say, "How can you say such things about Mother Lange?" I know this because if you are a follower of Jesus and want to be like Him, those are the things you do.

A WOMAN OF PRAYER

(Free Verse)

Hurry to the Blessed Sacrament
Unabashedly oft heard to speak
Give God His glory in contentment.
Pray for the world that we may all stay
Close to the Savior each blessed Day.

Loving Holy Presence was so dear
As she knelt daily to Him adhere.
Each moment spent became very clear
From her tight schedule to revere
As close as she could to cling so near.

Crosses became easier to bear
Knowing that Jesus was at her side
Nothing dissuaded or made her fear
Knowing that in Him she could abide
She took all things in her quiet stride.

MY PROTECTOR
HEARTFELT PRAYER TO GOD

Lord, you knew me before I knew myself.
Continue to know me
And if there is anything in me
That is not pleasing to you, my God
Pluck it gently out.
You chose me long
Before my parents came together.
Keep me on an even path
Lest I fall into the abyss.

Lord, you know me
Through and through
And you know before me,
What hurdles were in my path.
Guide my feet therefore, along
The straight and narrow way.
I know Lord that you
Have already helped me
On this journey of life.

Had you not been on my side
Where would I be today?
But you stood by my side
And guided my feet to higher ground.
It was You who gave me the strength,
The courage to keep on keeping on.
All through my life, Lord,
You were preparing me for this moment.

8

CRCRCRCRCRCR

Standing in the Breach

*"Thus I have searched among them for someone to build
a wall or stand in the breach before me to keep me from
destroying the land; but I found no one."*

—Ezekiel 22:30

The book of Ezekiel says that the Lord could find no one to stand
in the breach for him. Jesus came along and stood in the breach by
giving His life on the cross for us. Then Mary Lange came along and
decided that She too would emulate Jesus. She said to herself and to
Jesus, "Here I am, Lord, I will stand in the breach for you," and so she
did. It was not easy trying to keep out the enemies, but relying on the
Lord, she stood steadfast in her resolve.

By making that promise, Mother Mary Lange made a huge
difference in this world. Each of us can do the same. We do not have
to make a grandstand. Jesus, our Savior, came to set us free, to be the
best that we could be. Jesus stood in the "breach" for us. Mother Mary
Lange during her lifetime also stood in the "breach" for her people.

Are we willing to stand in the "breach" for others? Standing in
the "breach" is no easy task. It takes steadfastness and resilience to

stand in the "breach." Many of the saints took the stand of standing in the "breach" for others. Some even paid with their lives for Christ to continue their stand.

We cannot hope to stand in the "gap" for anyone, if we are not steeped in the knowledge and love of Jesus Christ. Standing in the "breach" means letting oneself be duped by Christ, to be used by Him, to be an earthen vessel. We must have a deep, deep personal relationship with Christ to stand in the "breach." We have to literally fall in love with Jesus. That is some radical theology. Falling in love with Jesus . . . think about it. We hear of people falling in love with a man or a woman but not falling in love with Jesus. But if we want that deep, deep abiding love for Jesus, that Lange had, we must literally fall in love with Him. Not that mushy, clingy, lustful love but that "agape" love. That pure unadulterated love that will last forever and ever . . . that God love . . . that forever love. Mother Lange had this kind of love for Jesus.

Standing in the "breach" means that you are willing to be talked about, maligned, and mistreated. People will think they are doing you a favor just to have you wash their clothes, make their beds, or shine their shoes. Some will even call you ugly names and throw racial slurs at you and expect you to like it. You put up with it for the sake of the kingdom. When Mother Lange endured some of these things, she knew that Jesus was with her just as He was with the saints when they were persecuted. Standing in the "breach" is no easy matter, and one has to be prayed up at all times to do the work of the Master in a rude and ruthless world.

Although a highly educated woman, she did what had to be done to feed her sisters and the children in her charge. No work was beneath her. God rewarded her with the strength needed to undergo many hardships and difficulties in her life and that of the early foundation of the congregation. When times were hard, she forged ahead and stood firm and steadfast in the "breach."

Mary Lange was a good student who followed the example Jesus taught her by His stance in being steadfast in holding the breach by His death on the cross. She knew that just as Jesus held the "breach" and conquered death, she too, in following His footsteps, would be able to hold the "breach" and earn a place with Him in heaven. Are you willing to stand in the "breach" like Mother Lange even in these modern times for what you believe? As stated in the beginning of this message, it is no easy task unless you are all fired up for and with Jesus.

JESUS STOOD IN THE BREACH

Jesus, you stood in the breach for us all
Allowing us your children to stand tall

As we contemplate your great sacrifice
Meditating on the cost and great price

As you died on the cross in our stead
So that on your flesh we are daily fed.

Jesus, you stood in the breach for us
So that we could follow you thus.

LIFE BEARABLE

(Double Butterfly)

Life is bearable
When one takes time
To be still,
Listen
And hear
What God wants
Them to do now,
With their lives today.

=============

Mary Lange listened
Gave God her life.
Forever
To mold
To use
As He willed
Until they met
At her journey's end.

9

CRUSCRUSCRUSCR

All for the Glory of God

"Do all you can for the glory and honor of God."

—Mother Mary Lange, OSP

The above statement was written by Mother Lange to a friend. She could well be saying the same thing today to us her sisters and friends. From what is known by her actions as she lived it while a sister, the above statement was probably something she said often. As people of God and as people who are striving for a closer union with God to be authentic children of so good a Father, we must always do everything for the honor and glory of Him.

One can assume that Mother said the above statement, "Do all for the honor and glory of God," often. If she did not say it, she must have thought it as she went about her daily task. We today would call it having a special relationship with God, being intentional. Seemingly,

Mother Lange had many occasions to say that phrase. Life was not easy in those days, so staying close to Jesus and doing all for him was paramount in her life.

Life was not easy in Mother Lange's time. There were no washing machines, dryers, electric or gas stoves, dishwashers, air conditioners, or other amenities—conveniences everyone in our society takes for granted today. Can you envision no concrete sidewalks and all that mud on rainy days? Yet in spite of this, she still relied on the Lord for all her needs. There were more important things to think about, but then she did not know about the conveniences that we know about today. How could she have missed something she never had? If she had them, her reaction would have been the same. She would have been free, being herself, doing all for the glory of God.

The times in which she lived were not easy. Because of financial woes, she did what she had to do to keep her school and community solvent. She did not think it below her to wash, iron, and clean for others outside of the convent. She really had to keep her spirit up, relying solely on the Lord. That is one of the reasons Mother Lange is so admired today. Life for her was indeed hard, but she made the best of what she had. Today we would say that sometimes God sends us lemons and if we are resourceful enough, we make lemonade. Mother Lange made many pitchers of lemonade during her lifetime. Thus, her little congregation, with the assistance of dedicated sisters and friends, was able to survive.

Mother Lange knew that God was always at her side. That she was truly a woman of Providence was evident throughout her life. Providence did provide for all her needs. Mother Lange could have thrown up her hands and given up, but she hung in there doing all for the honor and glory of her God. She must have thanked God each night for another day gone and praised Him for the beginning of another day.

Mother Lange has given us examples to follow. The main one is to lean on God and do all for His honor and glory. At the end of the day, we will not be sad because "we messed up," but we can wake up each morning anxious to begin another day to offer God our praise and honor. God rewards all who put their hope in Him while trying to live a holy and unselfish life.

RISK TAKER

Mother Lange was unafraid
She was a risk taker.
Knew God would come to her aid.
She was not a faker.

Would lay down her life for justice.
Unafraid of those bounty hunters.
Obedient to God and . . . cool as ice,
As she faced all her mockers.

A no-nonsense risk taker,
Ran the gamete with naysayers.
Confident in fervent prayer,
Had no time for tale bearers.

EXAMPLE FOR ALL

(Blank Verse)

Mary Lange left us good examples.
She wrote nary a book or booklet,
Yet her name still resounds.

In all situations . . . prayer was her sword
Nothing daunted her spirit . . . her determination.
Relying on Providence, she did all things well.

And so she persevered . . . so can we,
As we follow the footsteps of this woman,
On our journey to the Promised Land.

10

ෆ෨෫෨ඬ෨ෆ෨

Mother Mary Lange . . . "A Christ Bearer"

Each day she carried Christ's Word in her heart
Touching each sister and brother
In her daily walk.

When the "Word" was implanted into the heart of Mary Lange and her being acted upon this "Word," the process of personal commitment began. God was so good to her and through her to all Oblate Sisters of Providence. Because of the Word made Flesh, we are all free to call God Father, who loves us and provides for all our needs. Mother Lange knew that our responsibility is to respond to the Word in a positive manner. She lived her life with eyes fixed on the Word.

To respond to God's Word, she knew that her heart must be open to the heart and mind of God, be faithful to the teaching of the Word who dwelt among us. Hanging on to the teachings of the Word, her world of "self" had to change. And change it she did. Lange's life became a total oblation to God. She learned to become all things to all people. It must not have been easy for her in the type of environment she found herself in the early 1800. Her example to become "A Christ Bearer" was not easy, but if we do things for God, it becomes easy through love for the Lord. Her focus was that of Christ in all aspects of her later life.

Walking in the Light of Jesus

Jesus told the apostles, "You are the light of the world, a city set on a hill cannot he hidden" (Matt. 5:14). Jesus was not speaking to the apostles only but to all of us who embrace the Christian life, that is to all baptized persons. Jesus was telling us that wherever we go, we must be lights, lights to each other, our neighbor, the orphan, the elderly, the youth, and all people we encounter daily. Mainly, He was talking not only about our examples to others but also about the use of our time and talents to anyone who needs enlightenment.

Mother Lange and the first sisters were definitely lights to all they encountered. Education was one of the ways they used for spreading their light. They opened the minds of girls and boys, men and women, and broadened the horizons of people they encountered in tending the sick, giving shelter to the homeless. They were a light to the city of Baltimore then and are still a light to this day. Being light allowed the sisters to go places only they dared to venture, to do things that many thought impossible for people of color to do, especially colored women.

Mother Lange's lantern hung high in the city of Baltimore when she opened schools and orphanages. Later her sisters went to other states to shed this light Jesus told us we were. Mother Lange opened doors for those who came after her. She opened paths for others to follow. Her discipleship was authentic. The light that God gave her was a useful tool so others could see a better way to live.

The Oblates through the effort of Mother Lange and our early sisters are trying to keep the light Jesus talked about burning as we tend to the mission of the congregation. A true disciple must go out with full force, being unafraid to spread the message of Jesus, to light the world with truth and righteousness. We are admonished to spread our light through the Good News so that all we meet—black, white, brown, yellow, and those in between—can be nourished by the encounter.

UNIQUE LOVE

Mother Mary Lange loved God,
In a very unique way
Left everything to serve Him
So radically.

At times it was very hard,
To be so kind and loving,
When the road was so bumpy,
And so unloving.

She stood firm by her great faith
In the providence of God's
Grace and mercy to see her
Through . . . to journey's end.

MEDITATION

Mother Lange took time to pray,
Took time each day to meditate
To be in communion each day
With the Master, teaching her His way.

It was here at deep prayer and reflection
That Mary Lange learned the art
Of the interior life after the Master's correction
Infusing the light of His life into hers.

Mother Mary Lange passed this act
Of interior prayer to her sisters
To their union with the Lord
Would be their bulwark in hard times.

11

"Servant of God," Mary Lange, OSP

Many would like to see "Venerable" or "Blessed" but most of all "Saint" in front of Mother Lange's name, as do we who love her. Mother Lange was always a silent woman who left little writing because she was such a humble woman. We do not know what pact she has made with God, but it could be that they have come up with the idea that things will be done in God's own time, not ours.

We who know and love Mother Mary Lange are confident that she is a saint already. All we need to do is continue what we are doing and let God do what God is going to do. Let us continue to make her known and loved through whatever means are out there. God who performs miracles every day by rising before the sun will make a way out of no way that will lead Mother Lange to the "altar of sainthood." Everything that needs to be done is being done, and so we wait! Let us remember that God is God, and being God, He does not think like us. Everything is in God's hands at the moment, and sainthood will happen when it is time. In the meantime, let us continue to pray and imitate Mother Lange in our daily lives. God hears all prayers; His answer to us today is "Now is the time."

Even when Mother Lange is declared a saint, she will still hold the title of "Servant of God." That is what she longed to be all her religious life, a servant of God.

A PRAYER

To Mother Mary Lange

Mary Lange, Servant of God
We ask your intercession to God
To grant our petitions.

We know that you loved all the
People of God especially the marginalized
And those with no one to care for them.

We know that while you were on earth
God listened to your every prayer
We know he will do so now as well.

Ask God to bless your Oblate Sisters,
Send them vocations, bless all the children,
Especially orphans.

We beg you to ask the Lord for peace
In the world, peace in our hearts
And a love for Jesus.

May our lives be an open book so that
God can use us as He used you
To further the kingdom of God.

We humbly await God's most
Gracious reply to our petitions.
Amen.

COME . . . WALK WITH ME

Come,
Mary Lange,
Take my hands.
Let us walk through
The quiet garden of rest.
Where troubles are no more,
No stress . . . nothing but peaceful rest.

Come,
Walk with me,
To the clear water of blessed repose.
Where refreshment is plentiful,
Where you can drink until full.
You'll thirst and fret no more.

Come,
Think with me,
In the quiet shady forest
Through calm paths of peace,
Of tranquil silence;
Where love, peace, and joy abide.

Come
Walk with me
And rest, my child . . . whispers the Lord,
Come!

SAINTS IN STAINED-GLASS WINDOWS

(Free Verse)

Saints in stained-glass windows
Are a wonderful sight to behold in our time
When the sun shines through, they live in our minds,
Saints in stained-glass windows

Saints in stained-glass windows
Worked diligently, we're told, for the Lord apart
Who took their task each day to heart,
Are now saints in stained-glass windows.

Saints in stained-glass windows
Set an outstanding example for all to follow
Working for God even now . . .
in their space so hallow
These wonderful saints in
stained-glassed windows.

Saints in stained-glass windows
Beaconing all to follow the Lord of all
The reward is great if you do not falter or fall
To become a saint in stained-glass windows.

Saints in stained-glass windows . . .
One day we'll see our Mother Lange's frame
With the word "saint" in front of her name
A saint in a stained-glass window.

Made in United States
North Haven, CT
31 January 2023

31924795R00043